D1241432

# 13/13

## Vietnam: Search and Destroy

THE WORLD PUBLISHING COMPANY
*Cleveland and New York*

# 13/13

*Vietnam: Search and Destroy*

*by Gordon Baxter*

Dedicated to
the men of India Company,
3rd Battalion,
1st Marines

Published by The World Publishing Company
2231 West 110th Street, Cleveland, Ohio 44102

Published simultaneously in Canada
by Nelson, Foster & Scott Ltd.

First World Printing 1967

Printed in the United States of America.

# Contents

# Glossary of special terms

Amtrac—a small, open, armed amphibious vehicle with tractor treads, used for ship-to-shore operations and on land.

Charlie—a slang name for the Viet Cong.

ECM—electronic countermeasures — radar jamming devices, and equipment of a similar nature.

KIA—killed in action.

MAC-V—Military Assistance Command-Vietnam.

MedCAP—Medical Civic Action Program. Teams of military doctors and medical corpsmen who are sent to treat the Vietnamese in villages that lack medical facilities.

Medivac—medical evacuation teams, transported by helicopter, which pick up the wounded and transport them to base hospitals for treatment.

Ops—Operations Department.

PF—Public Forces, local South Vietnamese militia. The South Vietnamese regular army forces are called "Arvins," derived from RVN, abbreviation for Republic of Vietnam.

13/13—thirteen casualties on February 13, in the course of a search-and-destroy mission.

USIA—United States Information Agency.

VC—Viet Cong.

# Introduction

Putting aside American vital interests and the honoring of treaties, we must remember that we are also in Vietnam for humanitarian reasons. There are people there . . . be it one million or three million or ten million . . . who were heard crying out for help. We responded, along with the Australians, New Zealanders, Thais, Filipinos, and the South Koreans.

Secretary of State Dean Rusk has said it over and over: "We are in Vietnam to help establish a climate in which peoples and governments will let other peoples and governments alone."

Even though that statement may run the risk of over-simplification, it is nonetheless an accurate description of our program and intent in Southeast Asia. This will be a more stable and secure world if and when the expansionist governments of Asia are made to understand that their ambitions cannot be realized by the use of force.

It is, indeed, arguable whether the vital interests of the United States extend as far as the 17th parallel in Vietnam. However, the North Vietnam government and the Chinese Communists have asserted that if South Vietnam could be seized,

7

the next targets would be Thailand and Malaysia. That represents a threat to our vital interests and it activates the military-aid sections of treaties in which we promised to protect these peoples from outside aggression.

Indirectly, the Chinese Reds are the enemy in Vietnam. They can read a stern lesson in the firm implication that the United States is not prepared to stand by and look the other way while they carry out their stated designs and ambitions in the Far East. The warning to China is clear: she must come to peace with the rest of the world and cease being the international rowdy.

Directly, however, the enemy is the North Vietnamese Communist and his lackey, the Viet Cong. Even at this late date, when we have suffered well over five thousand fatalities in the fighting, it is not sufficiently understood that the North Vietnamese Reds have scientifically developed and perfected the art of guerrilla warfare. This development threatens to be one of the most significant events of this century. Its grim meaning is that a small country, no bigger than North Vietnam, can launch a powerful military effort . . . powerful enough to challenge even the United States. The skills of this type of warfare were exported to Algeria, and the French fell victim to it for a second time. Earlier they had been defeated by it in Vietnam. The Chinese and the North Vietnamese have said that they intend to employ this new kind of warfare to write a new order for the world. We have challenged it.

But the American military forces in Vietnam, from General Westmoreland to the newly arrived private, agree that the final decision cannot be made by military means. It will depend upon the South Vietnamese themselves. Our military effort has more than just one goal. Primarily it is aimed at buying time and opportunity for the South Vietnamese to enable them to form an effective, just, and efficient government that will in the end succeed in knitting their society together.

It is not a hopeless prospect. In spite of the fact that about half of the fifteen million South Vietnamese are illiterate, the people of South Vietnam are sufficiently sophisticated to appreciate the benefits of peace and good government. Having elected their village leaders for several generations, they understand the democratic processes. The country is potentially rich. With a few years of peace and effective government, it could prosper.

This task of "nation building" is going on and is being undertaken in the midst of the fighting. The American contribution to this "nation building" is called "Civic Action." It was introduced by the men of the United States Marine Corps and is now practiced by all branches of the military in Vietnam and by hundreds of American civilians. In many respects, it is the larger effort of this war. The number of hours any soldier spends in combat are limited, but he spends thousands of hours in building roads and irrigation canals and bridges, constructing schools and hospitals, picking up children, caring for war refugees, and protecting people from the sickening brutality of the enemy. The American fighting man in Vietnam is helping win the hearts and minds of the people for a new South Vietnamese government.

Gordon Baxter has clearly become committed to this extraordinary and unprecedented effort of the American fighting man in Vietnam. His eye and ear are sharp and accurate. His pictures and his comments represent a valuable contribution to an understanding of what it is the American soldier is doing in that faraway land. The soldier knows, but too many citizens here at home do not.

Gordon Baxter's commitment to the American effort in Vietnam is apparent in his generous decision to pass on to the Marine Corps Reserve Civic Action Fund for Vietnam a share of his royalties from this book. By the way, that fund, which is administered by CARE, and which has been raised primarily through contributions from Marine Reservists, has now reached almost half a million dollars.

*Chet Huntley*

# Vietnam: Search and Destroy

# Prologue

When I arrived in Saigon, my first stop was at the Joint United States Public Affairs Office. They asked me, "What kind of news are you working?"

I said, "Put me in contact with the enemy." I have always felt the essence of reporting a war is to go where the shooting is.

The MAC-V officer laughed and said, "You reporters have just two kinds of trouble. You can't find enough war, and then you find too much of it."

A few days later he dispatched me north to Da Nang to join the Marines in Operation Double Eagle.

This story is uncensored. I did not receive a guided tour. I was free to take photographs of anything I saw. The American military officers and the South Vietnamese government gave me carte blanche; none of them asked to see or censor my material.

I knew I wanted to see a war; I did not really know where my political convictions lay. I know now, but want only to reveal them to the reader through the story of what I saw and what I photographed. Sometimes I feel I may have lost perspective because my story was taken as though a powerful magnifying glass had been laid upon the map of Vietnam, south of Da Nang, to bring it closer and closer to the eye, to the point of losing total perspective and being caught up in fascination with the grossly enlarged details of a very small area. This is not a "Report on the War in Vietnam." It is a painfully accurate, close-up study, narrow in scope. Everything is here as it happened.

Perhaps, after you have looked and read, you will understand a little better. The results of the war in Vietnam will be felt all over the world, especially in those places where Communist power has resulted in partition or so-called neutrality, as in Germany and Korea.

G.B.

# A Time and A Place

We lost 13 good men on the 13th day of February, at the base of a mountain, in the village of Tha Binh. This action was little more than an incident; it didn't even make the dispatches. But for me, and the people of that village, and for India Company, 3rd Battalion, 1st Marines, it is a time and a place to remember.

Pan Am flies a regular schedule from San Francisco to Saigon. The flights are crowded with replacements. The usual complement is ninety men, jetting off to war, dining on Rock Cornish hen, listening to light classical music in stereo, or watching a Doris Day movie. It takes very little time to go from San Francisco's International Bar to the Tan-Son-Nhut airport in Saigon.

15

The approach to the airport is high and steep in order to avoid small arms fire from around the field. On my plane, the Pan American captain announced, "I hope I can fly with you again, another day, under better circumstances." As we landed, jungle-bound recruits took a last look at the civilized interior of an American jet plane and a lovely blonde stewardess waving good-bye from the cabin door.

It's natural enough, when you are in a war-torn country, to want to know where the front is. It was my first question when we landed. I was not prepared for the answer. The MAC-V officer said, "You're at the front now. You were at the 'front' the minute you stepped off that plane. One of the first things you'd better learn about this war is that there isn't any front or any rear. The Viet Cong are all about us, among us—a part of us."

Despite the frequent mortar attacks and terror bombings, the personnel at the Tan-Son-Nhut airport takes a business-as-usual attitude. Souvenirs continue to be sold; civilian aircraft keep the traffic lanes busy; Asians, elderly and otherwise, continue to come and go, unperturbed by screeching Phantom jets, bristling with rockets.

17

There is nothing to prepare a newly arrived American for the sights, the sounds, or the smell of Saigon. An Oriental-French city, a Paris of the East, an open sewer, it is a city apart, unique and distinct from the rest of Vietnam. It is the political and economic capital. Since it is the seat of the government, it is politically important but it by no means represents the rest of Vietnam. It is, instead, the singular, strategic city of a rural backward nation. Saigon, with the twin city of Cholon, has two million inhabitants, of whom three hundred and fifty thousand are Chinese in origin, twenty thousand are Europeans, and five thousand are from other Asiatic countries. Living there, one becomes conscious quickly of the average temperature of 84° with accompanying humidity. From March to August it's much like being in Washington, D. C., in midsummer, for that is the hottest period of the year. The traffic is fantastic, with thousands of motor scooters, bicycles, three-wheel rickshaws, and six thousand Renault taxicabs (of which more later). Crossing a street is an adventure in itself.

18

Even in peacetime, Saigon would be dangerous. In wartime, it is a city of terror. Poverty and its sister, crime, are everywhere. In one sense, during this war, it is an open city. Men on leave, from *both sides,* go to Saigon.

I asked one of the military, "Who are the VC?"

He answered, shrugging, "The taxi driver. The pedicab man. The guy at the bar next to you. The bartender." Every American stationed in Saigon knows that the VC can be anybody. He knows, too, that the same thing can be true in the villages. The saying goes, "Farmer by day, VC at night." Sometimes, a soldier's margin of personal safety can improve when he is stationed in a place over a period of time and makes friends.

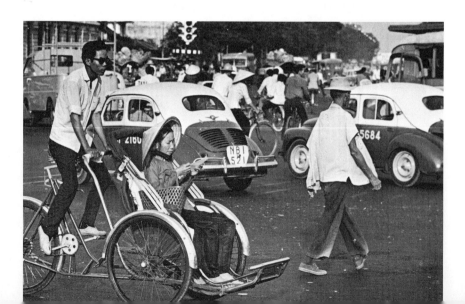

The seat of power is in Saigon, but that power has shifted many times since 213 B.C., when the Chinese invaded Vietnam and succeeded in subjugating the country. It took 399 years to do it, however—something we should remember. It was the Chinese who provided the name Vietnam, which means "the southern people." The country itself they called Annam, meaning "the Pacified South."

By A.D. 950, the Vietnamese had developed sufficient strength to rid themselves of the yoke of physical occupation by the Chinese. Later, in the fifteenth century, Kubla Khan successfully invaded Vietnam, but his rule lasted only a few years. After his withdrawal and until the mid-nineteenth century, Vietnam enjoyed virtual independence, marred only by payments of annual tribute, which the Chinese demanded and were strong enough to collect.

It was the French who entered the country unilaterally in 1863, as a result of the persecution and repression of western missionaries. By 1873, they had consolidated their ruling position over the entire country, and they maintained that control until World War II. Vietnam became part of French Indo-China together with Cambodia and Laos. As they had been when dominated by China, the Vietnamese almost always were in a state of revolt against the French, but, nevertheless, many traditional Vietnamese patterns of political, social, and intellectual life were weakened and changed.

21

Following the fall of France in 1940, the Vichy government acceded to the occupation of French Indo-China by the Japanese, who remained in control until 1945. During those five years, the Japanese promoted opposition to the French and spread their own philosophy of "Asia for the Asians." Also during this time, the Viet Minh evolved as the major opposition to Japanese control, and when the Japanese were defeated in 1945, Ho Chi Minh created the "Democratic Republic of Vietnam," claiming jurisdiction over all of Vietnam. By the end of 1945, he had consolidated his control over the northern half of the country. But in 1946 the French returned and regained control over most of the population centers. Their authority over the countryside was challenged by the Viet Minh, and after six months of fruitless negotiations the Viet Minh attacked the French on a wide front. The war lasted for eight years, ending in the defeat of the French at Dien Bien Phu. The Geneva Conference in 1954 divided Vietnam into two parts, and in July of 1954 Ngo Dinh Diem, a political unknown, was named to form a government over the sixty-five thousand square miles that lie south of the 17th parallel. By October of 1956 the Republic of Vietnam had become a political entity. With all the territory's history of change and revolt, it is not too surprising that the many factions which exist in the country today are also looking to their own future, each reaching for power, knowing that with the promised elections the country will once again be in the hands not necessarily of the majority, but certainly of those most effective and influential. Thus, the unrest continues even in the midst of war. And while no real solution is possible until victory has been achieved, the task of unifying the country and its beliefs is infinitely more difficult than that of merely winning the war.

Typical of the banners written in English for the benefit of the American photographers and the American reader is this one found by the Marines in the Quang Dong village area. Signs such as these abound in Saigon and often the men who carry them don't know what the words mean. In many cases, the sign carriers have no political convictions and perform a meaningless task.

Saigon is a city of paradoxes. Architectural antiquities stand beside newly constructed high rise buildings; political slogans, printed in a language unintelligible to the average native, float by on gaily colored banners; armed guards protect the rights of the Vietnamese as well as those of the Viet Cong. We pay for the armed guards and we must remember that without them the situation would be worse.

The merchants continue to thrive—and they earn their living from both sides. They don't want us to leave. The government, torn, fractious, forever wrangling, does not want us to leave. The peasants, the vast majority of simple people, do not want us to leave. Why should they? They vote with their feet. Nobody flees north.

Outside the Joint United States Public Affairs Office in downtown Saigon there are concrete barricades. They are an indigenous part of our defense against bombs. While the Viet Cong bomb crews are not as well equipped or as well trained as our SAC B-52 boys, they do have a highly effective bomber; this is a Renault taxicab that they fill with dynamite. One of these driven through the plate-glass front of your office can ruin an entire working day.

It's advisable to have a few ground rules for survival in Saigon. Mark Crocker of the USIA gave some to me. "Don't sit in the front booth at the bar. Sit in the back. When they roll the grenade in, it just gets the front customers. And don't stand in front of plate-glass buildings. When the bomb goes off it blows the splintered glass outward."

The contrasts in the city of Saigon are endless.
The beauty of the flower blossoms in the public
square catches you by day; the burst of bombs
and the thud of mortars are nighttime com-
panions. The stench and ugliness, standard
by-products of poverty, can overwhelm one, but
the beauty of Saigon's women makes an indelible
impression on the American fighting man. These
tiny, doll-like, perfectly proportioned flowers spe-
cialize in being feminine. There are few who mind
the price of their favors.

Stealing and selling are a natural way of life in a city of poverty. The black market flourishes and PX supplies contribute their share, but the situation is not as bad as it was in Italy during World War II—or, at least, the looting is not as highly organized. Street vendors scrabble for existence; no one can say they are not glad to be surrounded by American servicemen loaded with money in the middle of a currency system that is running wild.

Shopkeepers in Saigon come in various sizes. Sometimes a very young one minds the store for his father because he learned how to speak English in school, and if his family runs a typical modern shop, their profits will be tremendous. *Both* sides trade in these shops.

Below is a picture of a smiling young man. He is grinning because he has just cheated me. His daddy is smiling, too. Actually, daddy has had twenty years of smiling—he was equally successful at cheating the French before we ever got there. Like merchants all over the world, Saigon shopkeepers are getting along as well as they can, war or no war, and with any government that happens to be in business.

## The War

This war has spawned a new generation of American fighting men. They have their own slang and their own nonregulation gear such as a "go-to-hell hat." Shown here is Pat Loupe, Airman Second Class, from Port Arthur, Texas. At this writing, Pat, in his teens, has two Viet Cong kills.

He still has nightmares about it. He had killed two VC infiltrators and when he turned the bodies over with the toe of his boot, he saw that the VC were both in their early teens. It is not uncommon in the ancient history of Oriental wars to have the very young pressed into service.

Pat and the others in his outfit work with the K-9 Corps. These men and their dogs guard bases and airstrips at night.

Pat Loupe is in Vietnam to protect equipment. One of the planes on Pat's airstrip in Da Nang is a McDonnell Phantom, heavily camouflaged in jungle markings. The Phantom is an extremely successful airplane, used by the Air Force, Navy, and Marines to attack, bomb, and fight and for photo reconnaisance. Its ECM capability is extremely high.

Overnight a million dollars' worth of airplane can be reduced to hot junk. It's hard to defend an F-102 against one silent, practically naked infiltrator with a plastic bomb. It's hard to defend an air base against a swift three-man mortar team, particularly if the members of said team happen to be on your own payroll during the day.

We lose a lot of airplanes on the ground. The air-base people react calmly to the night mortar attacks and point with some pride to sniper bullet holes in their tents. Meanwhile, the ground crews work man-killing hours, and base perimeter security gets tighter and better.

31

At Da Nang, I asked the Air Force colonel in charge, "Why do we park our airplanes wing to wing? Doesn't that make them totally vulnerable —remember World War II? Couldn't they fly bombers in and hit us from Hanoi?"

The colonel said, "Yes, we remember and they could hit us. But this is a calculated military risk. Another paradox of this war. Remember we are guests here, and we can't get any more space than this. They'd rather grow turnips out there. We do more business off of one strip here than they do at Chicago's O'Hare Field, but one strip is all we've got. And, yes, they could hit us from Hanoi and wipe out this whole flight line, but they don't, and they won't. Because they don't want to escalate the war."

Another paradox of this war is that we had no off-the-shelf hardware available to do the right job. Airplanes advanced steadily after World War II: they grew heavier and faster, and when the time came to get down into the valleys and along the mountainsides, we didn't have anything that would do it. So we reached back and found the old Skyraider. This was the Navy AD, an attack airplane designed during World War II and proven in Korea. It's a tough airplane, able to absorb a lot of ground fire and carry its own weight in armament. It came out of mothballs and has been a big success.

The Navy had all of them but has now issued them to other services. I asked a jet-trained Air Force pilot, "What's the hairiest thing about a mission in one of these?" He said, "Landing it."

Speaking of old airplanes, the "Gooney Bird" is still with us in this war, after so many wars. These are the old durable DC-3's or C-47's. Some are being flown by crews younger than the airframes.

A gun-bus is pictured below. Those are revolving rifles, triple Gatlings, shrouded, that poke out the broadside gunports and look very much like the guns on "Old Ironsides." These planes are used when a heavy concentration of VC is located, or a fortified hamlet is about to be overrun. The pilot comes in low and slow, in a steep banking turn, and pours a withering cone of fire right down the wing spar—18,000 rounds per minute.

The guns are fired by the pilot, but young gunners keep the revolving barrels fed, clear jams, and collect a stunning number of Purple Hearts.

They take a lot of hits and suffer a lot of casualties. They call their plane "Puff, the Magic Dragon."

Among the most shot at airplanes in Vietnam are the C-123 transports. They have been converted to spray rigs for defoliating the jungle at altitudes of fifty to one hundred feet. At this writing, there were four of these birds. Three of them, "Patches," "Miss Susan," and "Little Devil," had a total of five hundred bullet holes, and their crews had earned seven Purple Hearts. The fourth, "Leper Colony," had a red patch over each one of its two hundred bullet holes and six Purple Hearts among the crew.

It's a war of contrasts. A young airman based in Vietnam enjoys three square meals a day, a first-class Base Exchange, and clean clothes. He comes to work each morning on his own Honda. He is living in what is almost the equivalent of a typical stateside air base environment. But when he gets to his "office," he spends his hours sweating, being shot at, and working camera and radio as observer in the little Cessna O-1. His is a forward observation plane or a spotter for air strikes and artillery.

It's hard to forget what one of these boys said to me. "Sir, what this aircraft lacks in fire power, it makes up for in slowness."

In many ways, this war reminds me of the winning of the American West. The terrain is rugged and crawling with the enemy. Our aim is to push the enemy back North, back onto the reservation. And, as in the winning of the West, there is a special vehicle involved. Our pioneers had the stagecoach; we have the helicopter. It goes where nothing else can go; it does the job when nothing else can do it. Rough, noisy, dusty, it's the indispensable carrier of any load and it's one of the most confounding devices that the Hanoi government has ever come up against.

The helicopter carries a man who rides shotgun. The crew chief of a "Big Charley" chopper is almost always cold because of the draft from his open window, often bored, and sometimes in extreme danger.

The M-60 machine gunners use two flak vests. They wear one like a vest. They fold the other one up and sit on it. After all, there is not going to be any incoming ammunition through the roof. And a young gunner can think about getting wounded in the shoulder, or hit in the leg, but. . . .

I will never forget my first look at the enemy. He was a captured VC—a little man with a blindfold on his face.

By tradition, by training, the captured Oriental has at the time of capture only one overwhelming thought in his head. He knows nothing of politics, except what his squad leader or political leader has taught him. He knows nothing about Americans and it is unlikely that he has ever looked at a magazine or newspaper. He is an Oriental soldier and he understands only that he has been captured. To him this means that he must wait for the beginning of pain ending inevitably in death.

If the roles were reversed it might be true. But since he is an American prisoner he will be interrogated, moved to a compound, and treated humanely as a prisoner of war.

# Operation MedCAP

The township of Loc Tan lies in the Quang Nam Province in the District of Dai Loc. I had not expected to visit it nor was I particularly interested in doing so. However, a colonel at the Marine Press Center in Da Nang, who would arrange later to have me join a combat outfit, suggested I go along on a MedCAP operation first. He said to me, "You may as well see another side of this war."

When we reached Loc Tan, it had just been secured. The VC had been pushed back about as far as the temple in the hills.

Most of the people of Vietnam live in small, isolated villages. There are no roads, no radios, no telephones, and no newspapers. Civilization has advanced very little since the time of Christ. Now, as then, a man who has traveled fifty miles is looked up to as a wise man.

The people don't know what's happening in Hanoi. They don't know what's happening in Saigon, or New York, or Moscow. The sum of their experience and knowledge is centered only on what is happening in their own village. When they see the "invaders" approaching their beach in amtracs, they send the women and children out to greet them. The men prudently stay out of sight.

The villagers don't understand world politics but they do understand local terror. In 1965 there were six thousand political assassinations. Now we come, apparently as yet another intruder. They await our actions with understandable reserve.

The people of the village of Loc Tan are farmers, hunters, and fishermen. They live much as they must have lived two thousand years ago. They are religious, affectionate, and secure in their way of life as long as they are free from the invader.

They have little use for money; they live by barter and trade in the village market. They are primitive, but not deprived. Their society is simple and well-ordered, and they are acutely aware that the invader from the North is among them. By our standards, they are uneducated, but they are content, with a philosophy as ancient as their culture.

The village streets were cool and shaded, and everything looked neat and clean. We came in past the market place and they watched us silently with veiled eyes. Some of the faces we saw staring at us were sullen and hostile. We knew that some of the men sitting in the shade of the huts were VC who would be fighting us that night. I had the distinct feeling that if I strayed out of sight of the Marine guns my body would never be found.

41

We set up a little clinic in the government house and our interpreters passed the word that the doctors and their medicines were here. These people who had never seen a doctor in their lives filled the square. I learned that this is a standard part of all our operations in Vietnam.

During Operation Double Eagle, Phase I, which covered an area of five hundred square miles, the Marines killed three hundred twelve Viet Cong and captured nineteen, while suffering fewer than twenty-five KIA and about one hundred twenty-five wounded. During the second phase of the operation, they gave nine thousand South Vietnamese medical attention, fed countless hungry civilians, and provided clothing where needed.

MedCAP operations can offer a great deal of variety and some are hard to resist. For instance, during a MedCAP session at the village of Chu Lai, Nguyen Minh Tung's eight-pound baby was delivered by Hospital Corpsman Third Class Gary Kunkel, USN, assisted by Marine Sergeant Lawrence McMahon. Hospital Corpsman Kunkel is holding the baby as his assistant and the baby's father look on.

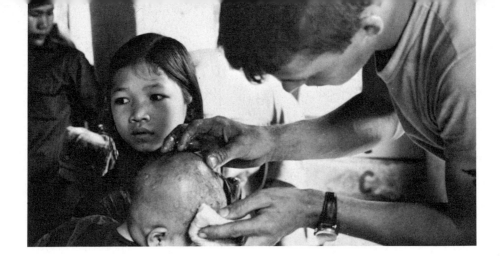

The Medical Civic Action Program is a vital factor in our operation in Vietnam. Few realize it exists, and yet President Johnson considers it second only in importance to the more immediate military program.

Our first objective in Vietnam is to bring the people security and to bring them freedom or safety from the Viet Cong who are overrunning their country. Our second objective, as demonstrated in the MedCAP operation, is to help bring the people of Vietnam into the twentieth century by giving them the medical care and civil help they need. The people of Vietnam want our help and they are getting it.

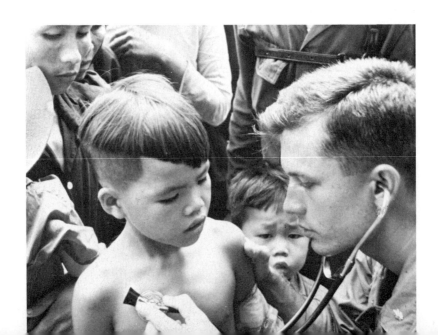

This aspect of our program in Vietnam is not publicized because it doesn't make good copy. It isn't sensational enough.

Americans have a natural affinity for children. The affection of the good American for the trusting native child is known to people all over the world. In Korea, the GI's themselves built orphanages for children. In World War II, there were few soldiers who could resist the waifs in Italy. We get along with kids. They steal our hearts as well as our wallets.

The doctor found a lot of tuberculosis. He called it the "international disease of the poor." He found a great deal of malaria and innumerable untreated insect bites. These people have no way of combating infection, and even insect bites can be dangerous and sometimes fatal.

The doctor felt that the villagers had a fairly good diet, but he pointed out that what the kids needed most of all was soap. That is exactly what this little fellow with the scared eyes fears he's about to get out of the Marine helmet. And he's right.

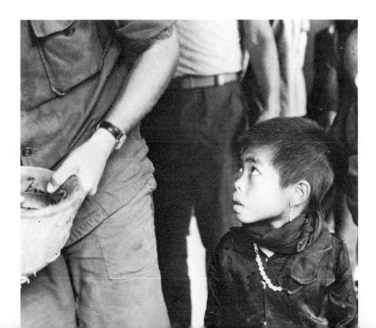

The native women of the village of Loc Tan have nothing in common with scientific young Americans. They have neither religion, language, nor culture in common. But when the child of one of these primitive women is sick, a bond is formed. At first, the doctor is looked upon with fear and apprehension. But when the doctor has finished, there is gratitude and trust.

Few idealistic missions are without flaws. Typically, even during a MedCAP operation, the enemy is everywhere. A kindly Marine handing out food to hungry children isn't apt to be aware that some of their playmates are at the back of the buildings busily stealing all the movable weapons and ammunition they can get their hands on. Native children don't think there is anything really wrong with this kind of stealing. They are stealing our ammunition for daddy, who's away, fighting in the hills, on one side or the other.

Primitive people can become quickly acquainted with the American Way of Life and our Great Society. We had a complaint one day from a lady who approached our captain filled with bitterness and bad news. The captain couldn't understand her so he called an interpreter.

The interpreter listened carefully, and then he said, "Captain, it seems as though, while we were defending this lady's plantation yesterday, that we shot down two very valuable coconut palms. And she wants to know, what is the United States government going to do about it?"

The United States government provides forms for the natives to fill out to request compensation for any damage we may have done to their fields or their homes.

48

When I saw some native soldiers, coming down from the hills, possibly to shift position and fight again that night, I asked our gunner about them. I said, "Gunny, are those our guys or their guys?"

Gunny said, "Tell you what you do. You get out there in the street and you aim your camera at them and if they don't shoot you, then they are our guys."

They turned out to be our guys.

There are many stories circulating about the South Vietnamese fighting men. Most Americans agree that the Vietnamese have one particularly strong characteristic; they won't get into a "no-win" situation. They have no compunction about running away to live so they can fight again another day. As far as they are concerned, that makes good common sense. They would never have had an Alamo; they do not believe in staying and dying for a cause. They won't try anything unless they are sure of winning.

Individually, the Vietnamese are likable people. They are handsome, chronically cheerful, and intelligent. They are family oriented, with much affection for their children. They are small, almost tiny people. A typical fighter is five foot two, one hundred and fifteen pounds, and built like a wiry junior high school athlete.

They are the kind of people who come swaggering out of a fierce battle, on their way to another fight, holding their carbines wrong end to, with wildflowers stuck in their helmets, and a grin on their faces. The whole company gave this hero catcalls as I photographed him, but he loved it.

They swagger off down the road, with a song on their lips, laughing, giggling, murderous little teen-age commandos. In this war there are tough, fierce little fighting guys, on both sides.

51

We left the little village of Loc Tan in helicopters. We took the medics back to the aircraft carriers and then flew up the coast a few miles, back to "Johnson City International," a dust-blown chopper base named for Colonel William G. Johnson, USMC, "mayor." This was the helicopter staging base for Operation Double Eagle, near Chu Lai.

The helicopter darted around a mountain and swept into a shaded green valley. Outposts watched us with upturned faces; the chopper barely touched, I bailed out running. When I stopped running, the bird had gone.

# Phase I

At the command post, Major W. D. Fillmore, 3rd Battalion, 1st Marines, shook hands briefly and pointed to the map he was holding. "We move out at midnight, march to this village at the foot of the mountain, take up position, attack at dawn, make a sweep of this village, and meet the 2nd and 4th Marines who will be blocking for us at the river beyond the village. You can go with Tim Lecky of India Company, or with Jim Sehulster, Lima Company. Better make up your mind and get with the men. It's nearly dark. Good luck."

The choice of war. Lima Company or India Company. Turn right or turn left. Live or die. I went stumbling off to India Company, with a cold feeling in the pit of my stomach.

Fifty yards away from the Command Post and across a clearing the Marines of India Company were nestled down. When I came up to Captain Lecky in the dusk and he saw that I was a reporter, he made an attempt at being cordial. "Welcome to our little patch of green," he said, indicating a grassy clearing in the brush.

There is no way I can bring back to life the exquisite fear that pervaded the jungle and the rice paddies around us.

The worst was the feeling of being alone. I felt very much alone despite the comfort of the Marines bedded down beside me, the soft voices in the night, and the murmur of men sleeping in

53

the open. Now and then, I heard a light cough or smelled a breath of cigarette smoke, and every so often the patrols up on the hillsides made contact and there would be the pop of a carbine and the bark of an M-14. My ears fanned out and my head acted like a radar set, turning constantly. They were contacting the VC all around us. The night was alive with them.

At about 10 o'clock in the evening, the shooting picked up and it began to rain. Flares popped high in the sky, lighting up the clouds, to settle softly onto the rain-soaked ground. Heavy artillery shrieked overhead and crumped into the hillsides. The shells came in fours, descending like notes of coming death.

I heard the impact of the shells about the same time that I could hear the guns go off on the coast.

"Gunny, what are they doing?"

"Killing cows."

"Well, what's all the action about out there?"

"It's just the 10 o'clock show. Charlie will keep it up about an hour or two, then pull back. Every night, same thing."

I lay on the stony ground thinking. "Nobody here even knows my name. They are trained for this; they know each other. Some of us will be dead at this time tomorrow or minutes from now. Is this the time? The place? I don't even know what part of Vietnam I might die in. What is that in the brush? The VC is the world's best night infiltrator. God, I'd hate to be captured. I think I heard something move in that brush. . . ."

I moved over to sit closer to the gunnery sergeant.

"What's the trouble, sir?"

"Gunny," I said, "I'm chicken." No answer.

As I sat there in my rain suit with sweat trickling down the inside and cold rain outside, I continued to think about death.

The gunny had rigged up some kind of a shelter out of stuff from his pack. I had the impression that he was lying in there cool and dry, no more perturbed than a man sitting on his front porch and watching it rain.

I thought about the midnight attack and wondered how late it was. My watch dial looked like a luminous skull. I thought about the swift passage of time, about the transient nature of the frail flesh of mankind. I thought about the Asian continent. There are tigers here, and elephants, and a large variety of poisonous snakes, spiders, and peacocks, and. . . . Then I began to laugh at the final extension of all the fear anyone can have. It isn't possible to sit up all night and be afraid of everything on the entire continent, is it? I thought of the faces of my family, and, like men in all wars, I took comfort in thoughts of home. Finally, a dead sort of sleep came.

The village of Tha Binh has a populace of 2,406 and is in the Phuoc Thanh Province in the District of Phu Giao. We planned a surprise dawn attack. The plot sounded like a movie classic. Move out at midnight, take up positions, go over the top at sunrise. Objective: the river. We were to reach the river and cross it alive. We would be among those who would wade out on the other side and we would be greeted by friends who had crossed ahead of us and were waiting for us now.

It made no more sense than a bad dream. In a close-knit, clannish valley such as this one, every man, woman, and child knew the Marines were there and they knew what we planned to do.

So we "sneaked" down the trail with the VC following along on both sides of us, fading in and out of the jungle to wait until we got to the place, the killing place. We came up the road and the enemy lay behind the logs and waited for us.

On the way, we passed through a friendly town, and an Army Special Forces man came out and had a quiet talk with Captain Lecky. He told us that they knew we were coming, and that they had a reinforced platoon in position to meet us. They would hit us going in, hit us on the left flank during the day, and hit us again as we were coming out. When he gave us this news, which was absolutely accurate, all but three of the PF's who were with us elected not to fight. They faded off toward home, padding away silently on little bare feet.

As we walked along, I could feel a gun muzzle tracking me inside of every jungle glade and in every dark-eyed window of a trailside hut. My neck bristled with fear. The three PF's who stayed with us guided us around many mines and traps that had been set for us. Their instructions were short and explicit. "Don't touch the fence. Pass it on. Mines. Stay in the center of the trail. Pass it on."

Some of the open-fronted huts in the jungle glades were at the edge of the trail. Families were sleeping in them, two and three in one hammock, and

men watched us in silence behind the dull red

dot of a glowing cigarette. Fear was in the air like a claw.

We had heard the gongs all night. First they echoed far away in the hills. Now they were closer, following us. They went, "long long long long-g-g-g," a doleful tubular metal sound. They were supposed to demoralize us, and as far as I was concerned, they sounded as if they were ringing my own personal death knell. They bothered Gunny Greer, too, but his approach was a little different. He told me, "We've captured all kinds of VC gear, but we've never found any of those gongs. I'd sure like to get me a gong."

And later, "I'll bet you they hang those damn gongs down in the chimneys. It sounds like it's coming out of a chimney. I'd sure like to take me a few men and go out there and get that goddamned gong. . . ."

When we were close to the village of Tha Binh, the women and children and the cattle began to come out. We were in a column of two's, and they came down the center of the trail, heads down, switching the cows along, shushing the kids. They were leaving the town, and they passed between the columns of Marines, "the invader," as they left. Not a word was exchanged. The smell of the fields, the hay, the cattle, the manure, and the countryside was heavy in the damp night. Little people, with great bundles of their things on their backs, hurrying to leave their town, passed right between our ranks.

When the ambush came, the enemy had pinned us down on a high trail that crossed the middle of a flooded rice paddy. Without warning tracers

57

were wandering in like fireflies. We stood there feeling naked on that high ridge road and it sounded like a Saturday night in the days of the Wild West saloons. I seem to remember that the cursing was louder than the gunfire.

We stood in ranks along both sides of the road. We were about 75 yards back from the head of the column where the hot fire fight was taking place. Then the VC hosed a string of tracers down the length of the column. We dropped down on one knee and knelt like crap shooters, playing, "I am as brave as you are, as you can plainly see." That is, all of us knelt except the PF's who had guided us here. They got way down off at the levee at the edge of the rice paddies. Then another burst sliced down the column keening into the dark and we went down flat on our bellies. I remember lying down behind a bulky Marine hoping to use him as a protective shield.

Captain Lecky had been trying to direct his men by radio to move up, but the head of the column was stalled in the cross fire. Finally, he went striding down the road, bellowing in a voice the men could hear over the gunfire: "Awright! I said 'Move OUT.' God dammit, you've got a whole company of men behind you. Do you want to keep this whole war to yourself?"

After we moved on up and came to the edge of the village, there was some confused wandering around in the paddies and the muck and finally we were in line, in position once more. The paddies were wet and muddy and it was raining again. One of the PF's was beside me, huddled.

I held up my rain suit edge and he crept over to lean up against me. In the jungle, during a night of terror, this fellow human and I, this unknown light tan Asian and I, warmed each other. This time I went to sleep quickly. I was not a stranger any more, not after the shooting.

It is dawn, and during the night the enemy has crept closer to us. Just as the sergeant said, "Let's saddle up and move 'em out," the shooting began. The bullets rippled through the banana leaves.

When the firing started, the sergeant shouted, "Awright, you guys, bunch up. Go on dammit, bunch up. You damn fools. The VC should get all of you!" Working in swift teams, and with blistering language, the noncoms got the men spread out and moving.

Crossing the rice paddy by early dawn light and
moving forward toward Tha Binh into the enemy
fire was bad, but it was not as bad as it had been
crossing the paddies in the dark last night. Now,
at least, we could see.

We could watch for the trip wires, for the mines,
and for the punji sticks. The punji stick, an extremely simple primitive weapon, is characteristic
of the Oriental. It is constructed from a bamboo
splint about eighteen inches long, with both ends
sharpened. One end is sunk into the ground; the
other is dipped in human feces. The VC hides
punji sticks in the weeds in low ground. If our
men are traveling over that ground in an action
and the VC opens fire, our soldiers belly flop into
the tall weeds. The punji stick is a simple but
effective weapon.

61

Our men couldn't move up fast enough. The VC were firing and falling back and our hard-chargers were working frantically to keep up the pace. The sergeants kept yelling, "Hold up. Get down. Get down you or I'll put a round over your head." But the sergeants always stand up.

The VC were firing and falling back, carrying their dead and wounded. The snipers picked away at us. A carbine would pop, and the rhythmic short bursts of a throaty M-60 machine gun would answer. We swept the brush and the hedgerows with slanting fire. They were shooting at men. We were shooting at sound.

The snipers placed themselves in high ground.
They were up in the trees, firing at us from
thatched huts. They kept picking away at us, but
did not effectively delay us. We took on some
wounded. But our own snipers found a few good
solid targets, too.

Shooting was heavy and we were taking on wounded. We knew VC were behind the houses or huts and that anybody running out of one of them could have been the enemy.

Any man running out of a thatched hut is suspect and becomes an automatic target. In this case an M-14 bullet took the top of his head off.

He was an old man and he was not armed. That's why he was left lying on the ground. He ran out of his house, holding our company up for a few precious moments, and two Marines were hit during the time it took to kill the old man.

It was not a time to stop and ask for papers.

With the stench of blood in our nostrils, mingled with the smell of wildflowers, we advanced through a Garden of Eden on a lovely spring morning. We moved forward as the birds and the bullets sang in the air around our heads.

Every valley, every smoke-shrouded vale, held its bite of death. A few moments of silence would be interrupted by the chattering roar of the machine guns. The gunner would fire from the hip with his teeth bared, cursing. Then the silence of the jungle would be with us again as we stalked on to pass a wounded man in the grass who would wink at us and motion us to go on.

At the center of the compound of huts they fought us man to man. It was here that a man had the knuckles of his hand shot away and the trigger mechanism blown out of his rifle. Automatically, he tried to shoot a triggerless rifle with a fingerless hand. Then he looked down and said, "It hurts. It hurts."

Another man was gut shot. His mouth formed a surprised O as he sat back heavily in the rice paddy in a widening pool of crimson.

We caught cross fire from the huts as we rushed
forward in the open space. We never knew where
the enemy would pop up next and we seldom got
a look at him. Without warning there would be a
flash, a zing, and a bullet had gone by. Nothing
can save a man here except chance. The random
fate of a bullet's flight is mixed with the gall of
fear and the feeling every soldier lives by: "It
won't be me."

A soldier does not want to be exposed. He knows nothing is more dangerous than running out into the open, up to a porch, to kick open a door and jump inside—into a dark hut. Anything can be in that hut: a waiting gun, a trip wire, or a mine.

The woman in the yard is ready to meet her death. As I ran through her patio, I stopped to take her picture. Her face has haunted me ever since.

She thought we had come to kill her and she faced that fact with infinite sadness and composure. In her mind, the invader was upon her. Her fields were afire, her flocks were scattered, and her men were gone. She came outside into her yard to exercise the last choice that any human being can have.

We are in Vietnam, fighting communism in this woman's back yard. If we did not stay here, we would appease and move back. We would appease and move back until at last we would be fighting in our own back yards.

Mortars give an infantry company a very heavy
punch. Both sides like to use them. Our people
also love the M-79 grenade launcher. It's like
brass knuckles in a barroom brawl. The only com-
plaints I heard about equipment concerned the
old-fashioned, heavy, tube-type radios. They are
bulky in the field and easily damaged. Outfits
luckier than ours were equipped with the new
transistorized sets.

As soon as the first mortar round dropped down the tube, the mortar outfit drew fire from the VC snipers. You would never believe the noise of a mortar, or the language it seems to require to operate one.

The machine gunners responded to the individual sniper who was harassing the mortar crew by cutting down all of the jungle around him.

This is called a "noise effect." I don't know how it affects the VC, but it bucks up our side.

The mortars are backed up by rocket launchers. With the cry "Fire in the hole," a great crash is heard and a puffball of smoke landing on a distant hut blossoms into red flames.

Rockets and mortars laid a barrage ahead of us, blasting strong points, blowing vast craters in the tender new rice in the river valley paddy.

India Company has come through the worst of it. The captain has directed his people to spread out, to sweep the paddies and hill slopes beyond the hut compound.

A spotter plane overhead told us that they were pulling back, carrying their dead and wounded with them, climbing up into the hillside and disappearing into tunnels. We moved forward up into the hillside brush. It was closed-in territory—so close that I felt the enemy could reach out and cut my throat.

We found the tunnels. Some of them were military tunnels, leading all the way back through the hills. And some of them were family bomb shelters, only a few meters deep.

There was no way we could tell what kind of tunnel each might be. So we blew them all shut.

Finally it grew quiet. All that was left of our action was the smoke drifting in the jungle valley of this little town.

The machine gunner turned and listened. All he could hear was the burning of the thatch.

The last Marine came across
the last rice paddy
in the rising heat of the day.

78

Our people had reached the river and regrouped.
A part of our mission was complete.

We fell out under the trees. The C-rations and
the water from the canteens tasted like steak and
champagne.

It was our first breather, the first time we had had to compare notes and to talk about what happened. We learned that, so far, we had one dead, eight wounded.

We learned about the near misses. One of our men, named O'Hara, heard his name called and turned his head. The bullet that would have gone into O'Hara's face and through the back of his head just creased his nose and tore away part of his cheek bone. O'Hara walked to the rear, holding his left eye up to his face with the palm of his left hand.

The Medivac helicopters came into the clearing
and picked up the wounded very quickly. One
tall kid was a ballplayer last year in high school.
If you happen to meet him, shake his left hand.

Ask *him* why we are in Vietnam. Debate Vietnam
with him. He knows, he can tell you. He's been
in touch.

A pitiful group came out of a burned thatch farmhouse. There were two dignified peasant women bearing a bamboo litter and the mangled remains of the man of their household, who had been wounded in the head. He was not going to live. There wasn't anything we could do. We tried to help, while his daughter watched in solemn quiet.

They went jogging off toward the river with their sad burden. I don't know where they went, or what they did, but I can't forget them either.

This scene is typical of any war, anywhere. A mortar shell has neither eyes nor judgment.

# Search and Destroy

They gave us orders to sweep back through the town again. They told us we had come through too fast during the shooting. This is the part I wish I had not seen and I asked the sergeant about it. He said, "Look, maybe you didn't get what this mission is all about. Our mission is to search and destroy and those words mean just what they say."

We had to go back now to search for weapons, for rice, for ammo; and to take all males prisoner. And to destroy.

The prisoners were politically interrogated. After questioning, the indignant old farmers went back to their farms and those whose politics seemed doubtful were taken to a compound for further questioning.

This is one of the fathers we captured. His little girl put her hands over her ears because she didn't want to hear daddy being shot. She has heard the rockets and the machine guns all morning and now she can't bear to hear her father being killed. But she can't tear her eyes away.

We treated the prisoner well. We took off his blindfold and let him carry his smallest boy piggyback. The little girl kept turning around and looking at me. I'll never forget her eyes. They were liquid with terror, like a helpless animal's eyes. She was sure we were taking all of them to a place to be killed.

Sometimes we were rough with the prisoners. I saw our men threaten a man at gun point and at knife point because he refused to come along.

The man shown here wouldn't get up. Our machine gunner has just slapped him out into the courtyard and laid his head open. He is still mad and wants to hit him again. But this is madness born out of combat. Our gunner glared at me, too, and at my camera, and said, "So? So I got eight buddies shot, and one in his grave. So what're we here for, huh? Teach this God damn gook a lesson!"

Another of our men is giving the prisoner cigarettes and a bandage. We confuse the Oriental. They underestimate both our savagery and our compassion.

Prisoners are much safer in the hands of the rear echelon, away from men still fired up by the heat of battle.

Meanwhile, we went on with our ugly business in the village. We went to the huts and found cows and pigs hidden down in the bomb shelters. We shot them. We laid waste to the land.

Our movements were swift and economical. A Marine would take out his lighter, reach up and set fire to the edge of a roof. The thatched huts burned brightly and we watched Vietnamese hand tools, cooking pots, and all their artifacts go up in smoke. The order of the day was, "Burn the damn gooks out. Burn it. Burn it, and they can't ever come back."

I asked the sergeant, "Why are we doing this? Why do we have to burn everything up?" The sergeant told me, "Listen. You hear that small arms fire? Well, it's not small arms fire; it's the ammunition burning in those huts. Ammo for the Charlies, stored in the haystacks, in the thatch. You ever spend a war hunting a cartridge in a haystack? Anyway, the follow-up guys will rebuild their thatches for them."

The sergeant pointed out toward the rice paddy. "See where they had stored the rice. Twenty-five 100-liter sacks of rice. Did you ever hear the old Asiatic saying, 'In this country, a grain of rice is ⟵ worth a drop of blood'? Nobody in this run-down village could afford that much rice. That was a treasure to the Cong."

This place was supporting the enemy. Either voluntarily or involuntarily. I don't know which, but I do know they won't do it any more.

We policed the area carefully because anything left might be useful to the VC. The gear that belonged to the man who was gut shot lies on the ground. That man was lucky enough to live.

The next man was not so lucky. He was killed
by the second round of rapid fire. The first shot
put a long crease in the metal of his helmet and
tore the cloth. The second round, coming at almost the same instant, put a little round dot in
his forehead.

We put the gear on litters and carried it out with us. The helicopters had already evacuated the wounded. We regrouped by squads again and moved out in open order, in silence, under the hot sun. We were finished here.

The long, winding file of Marines moved slowly along the rice paddies and down to the river again to ford it and to join up with friends on the other side. A tall young Marine ahead of me humped his pack, and began singing softly to himself, "Oh little Nellie, put your belly, right up close to mi-ine. . . ."

We felt good crossing the river. The water was cool and clear, the bottom was hard white sand, and the water washed the mud away. I felt almost normal again—as though I might live. As I turned around to take a pretty backlighted picture of the rocket squad and the prisoners, they hit us again.

Without warning, cross fire ripped into us. Once again we were taking wounded, hurrying on across the river. The VC had been hiding along the river's edge all the time, waiting. They had hit us going in, fought us all morning, and now they hit us going out, as advertised.

A white phosphorous bomb marked the suspected gun position of the VC behind us, as another wounded man was carried out of the river by his buddy. For a brief time they had half the outfit pinned down out in the open, on a sand bar.

A third man was hit, and carried on across. We were not running. We were crossing in good order. We were wading briskly but not running. I said to the captain, "What are you thinking about right this minute, honest now?" He said, "I'm thinking that I wish this river was deeper and I had a snorkel tube."

We came up onto the levee, where the friendly Marines were laying down a covering fire. Friendly fire, they called it. Actually, it was about the most dangerous thing we got into, all that friendly fire.

A man was hit on the levee, too. It seems that some VC had come out of this "secured" village and were working the levee with us, on our right.

We called on the artillery down at the coast for fire support and gave them the coordinates, locating the Charlie gunners. That quartet of 155's sounded sweet, coming overhead, singing in close harmony. They fired from gridded maps. We just gave them the numbers and they were right on.

And as though that were not enough, we called up Ops at Da Nang Air Base and they pushed the button on a pair of Phantoms that were sitting out there cocked, as they always are.

The Phantoms came shrieking down out of the overcast in a few minutes with napalm tucked under the wing and zapped the waterfront zone.

After that it was quiet across the river, except for the burning. The last squad left the sand bar and crossed the river in good order. Infantry, artillery, air strike worked together as a perfect team.

The wounded were laid out under the trees.

It is not enough to say I was grateful to the gunner I was with most of the day. The job he did with that M-60 machine gun keeping the VC off my behind answered a lot of questions.

Helicopters flew the wounded up to Da Nang to meet the hospital plane. The plane each day works its way up the coast, making all the stops.

Some of the men were already cleaned up and in hospital dress.

Some men had had enough sedative so that they wouldn't remember the long painful ride across the ocean to the base hospital in Manila.

Others were still in pain when they were put on the planes.

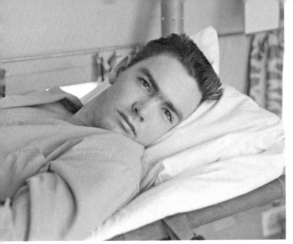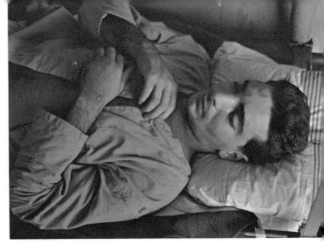
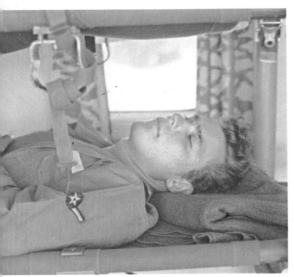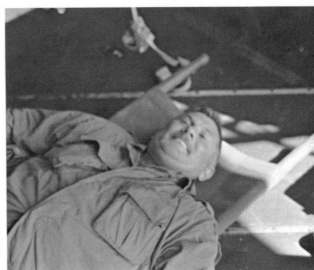

The superb dignity of men like these can never
be forgotten. Perhaps it is their training or a
sense of history that makes their pride endure.
Wounded, sometimes unto death, their dignity
shines through their faces, their eyes. Sometimes
a man just stares, but that stare can make lesser
men weep.

# The Buyers

We pay a high price for freedom; the freedom to write an uncensored book, the freedom to dispute a point of view. There is no guarantee that we can keep liberty. We have to buy it. Young men like these buy it for us. They understand what they are doing. It's surprising that so many people on this side of the ocean don't understand.

The excitement of the war comes and goes. In between, it means boredom and loneliness.

A fighting Marine lives out of a tight little pack, humped up on his back, for as long as necessary. His pack carries everything except C-rations and ammunition. These items come in by chopper.

104

The Marine shown here has been on his feet for twenty-four hours and he's been wet and dried out three times since the sun went down. His M-60 is almost too hot to touch because he's been in a fire fight twice this morning.

I talked to men of all ages, from toughened sergeants of fifty to raw young recruits. The answers to my questions were simple and straightforward. I asked, "What do we need most of all over here?"

"We need about four General Pattons."

"We need a President who doesn't think he can win a war by gaining a popular consensus."

Our men are tough and in good shape. I remember one who had had fourteen days in combat and watched his buddy die during a second round of rapid fire. I asked him how old he was. He said, "I'll be nineteen." Don't call them boys.

107

Without fail, every fighting man I talked to, at all ranks and levels, wanted to hit harder and move in faster.

A man in a reaction platoon is apt to spend his day in the broiling sun and sand, beside the helicopters. He is kept in reserve, standing by to respond to a call to support when an ambush occurs.

I asked this man, "What would you buy, if you had all the money you needed, and ten minutes to spend it in Sears?"

He said, "The salesgirl," and gave me a grin.

The men asked me questions, too. They said, "You just came from stateside. Are the draft card burners still at it? Has everyone in the country turned against the war now? Why don't they understand why we're here?"

I tried to answer them, sitting there on the beach, halfway around the world, at the edge of the South China Sea.

I said, "Let me tell you something. Those draft card burners defeated their own purpose. They woke us up. They brought about a resurgence of old-fashioned patriotism that this country has not felt since World War II and the bombing of Pearl Harbor. You're not fighting an out-of-town ball game in a dark stadium on a rainy night with empty grandstands. We are with you. Your country is solidly with you. Wait till you come home in that uniform. Just wait until you come home!"

When he comes home, he'll find out I lied to him.
But by then, perhaps it won't hurt so much.

# For the Record

The Seventh Fleet lies just off the coast, in the South China Sea. This fleet is capable of blockading Haiphong. The strength is already there. We also have supremacy of the air. We are in a unique military position, having these two vast strategic advantages over the enemy. Supremacy of both sea and air, and yet, at this writing, we haven't really used them both.

When I came back from Vietnam I asked why, at the Department of State. A very high-ranking official gave me a precise three-part answer, carefully held off the record. It was a deliberate, slowly spoken answer. My question was, "Why don't we blockade Haiphong?" and he said, "First, we are not yet ready to ask Russia to face up to another of our quarantines. Secondly, we are reluctant to bring up the many questions that will arise if we begin to stop the flags of other nations on the high seas. Thirdly, don't rule it out."

So for now this is a supply fleet, except for the carriers that launch those valiant air strikes to the North. This carrier is part of a fleet that moved a division of Marines in for the first real punch in support of the South Vietnamese government.

I remember that when the late President Kennedy first proposed this sort of response force, he was asking for jet troop transports and for task forces like this, to implement our policy of containment of Communism. He said then, "I want to be able to respond to the Communist threat anytime, anywhere, with any weapon from NATO to napalm."

We have the equipment that Kennedy wanted, and his policies are being implemented by President Johnson. The President has the flexibility of response and the ability to strike the controlled blow. He is able to apply enough pressure, but not too much, wherever needed.

We cannot abandon those men or these people. We are doing two things at once in Vietnam. Our reasons are both selfish, and altruistic. Our first objective is to maintain military security, to get the Communists out and to hold them at the border. Our second, to help the Vietnamese help themselves. Ours is, and must be, a policy of containment.

This means a new kind of war—a limited war. We strike controlled blows. We keep tightening the screws, until we convince the enemy that they cannot win. Only then will they be ready for peace talks. It is a matter of time.

And after that, what will happen? The Communists will doubtlessly challenge us in another place, in another way. We have put out two big and many small fires in the past twenty-five years. This is not as good as peace, or as bad as a World War III.

Our hope for Vietnam is that eventually it will learn to govern itself and will become a self-supporting, unified country. We will leave behind us permanent air bases and large ports, and we will try to provide this underdeveloped country with the means of moving ahead into the twentieth century.

Looking at it selfishly and realistically, the possibility exists that they may turn out to be neutrals, or even "un-easy neutrals," but the people of Vietnam will be caught up in the commerce of world trade, and they will become a part of a changing world of new growing nations. This world is one that we can live in better than the Communist can.

117

# Epilogue

This is only a small story. It is a personal account of an action on the 13th day of February 1966. We crossed a river and, at the foot of a mountain, we took a little village. We suffered twelve wounded and one KIA.

Do you still ask why? I remember what President Johnson said in New York City at the Freedom House Awards Dinner on February 23, just ten days after this happened.

''This is an American tradition . . . we will seek peace every day by every honorable means. But we will persevere along the high, hard road of freedom. We are too old to be foolhardy and we are too young to be tired.''

# Acknowledgments

With special thanks to these people who were vital to the completion of this assignment:
Jack Neil, owner, radio KTRM, Beaumont, Texas
Congressman Jack Brooks (Democrat, Texas)
Major G. B. Stevens, USMC (ret.)
Richard S. Stark

The pictures on pages 16, 18, 24, 25, and 28 appear through the courtesy of Wide World Photos, Inc. The pictures on pages 19, 20, 27, 46, 82, 112, 114, and 115 appear through the courtesy of Gordon Converse of *The Christian Science Monitor*.

120